The Bean Gourmet™ Presents The Greatest Little Bean Cookbook

THE BEAN GOURMET™ PRESENTS

The Greatest LittleBean Cookbook

Tom Chasuk

The Bean Gourmet™

Hearst Books / New York

Library of Congress Cataloging-in-Publication Data

Chasuk, Tom.
    The Bean Gourmet℠ presents the greatest little bean
cookbook / by Tom Chasuk.
      p.   cm.
    Includes index.
    ISBN 0-688-13765-2
    1. Cookery (Beans)   I. Title.
TX803.B4C44   1995
641.6'565—dc20   94-22838
                                             CIP

Printed in the United States of America

First Edition

1 2 3 4 5 6 7 8 9 10

BOOK DESIGN BY RICHARD ORIOLO

To the best mom and dad
in the whole wide world,
Dolores and Al,

and to my loyal goldfish,
Trent,
who has stood by me
through thick and thin

Acknowledgments

There are so many bean lovers out there who have been so very helpful.

Bill Adler, my great book agent, who has made my bean dream come true, and Julie Rosner for all of her help.

Megan Newman, my terrific, enthusiastic editor, who never knew how much she liked beans until she met me! And Megan's friendly, but now former, assistant Diana Capriotti.

My official bean tasters, who endured all of my recipe inventions: Annette Chasuk, Rebecca Cushman, Madeleine Cushman, John Chasuk, France Kirkpatrick, Nick Chasuk, Jack Chasuk, Anika Chasuk, Robert Chasuk, Patti Chasuk, Sam Chasuk, Daniel Chasuk, Patricia Boaz, Scott Boaz, Brian Boaz, Julie Boaz, Margaret Austin, Lonnie Austin, Jeanette Twa, Mike Twa, Emily Twa, Lisa Rose, Mike Rose, Philip Rose, Steven Rose, Howard Bender, Elissa Bender, Amanda Bender, Fletcher Bender, Stacy Dempsey, Lance Dempsey, Jeff Carew, and Steve Alvarez.

Some very exceptional hosts have been exceptionally kind. Steve Edwards and Cristina Ferrare, who gave birth to "The Bean Gourmet" on "AM Los Angeles," and Linda Dano and Dee Kelly, with whom I had a lot of fun for two years on their Lifetime show, "Attitudes." Thanks also to Jerry G.

Bishop and Kathi Diamant, Cyndy Garvey, Kathie Lee Gifford, Tawny Little, Tim Reid and Daphne Maxwell Reid, Susan Sikora, and Don Sanchez. And, of course, "The Late Bill Smith" for all the hours of fun on his hot radio show. And KMPC radio's Peter Tilden and Tracey Miller.

Special thanks to Steve Ober and Mary Ellen DiPrisco for giving me my first breaks on television. I also wish to thank the following producers who have been so supportive: Jack Anastasia, Randy Barone, Pat Caso, Barbara Chacon, Claudia Contreras, Patricia Elwood, Laura Gelles, Michael Gelman, Lisa Kridos, Lois Lee, Mimi Pizzi, Sue Podbielski, Diana Sabat, Roni Selig, Mike Stevens, John Tessier, John Verhoff, Margaret Weitzman, and Angela Wendkos. Many thanks also to KABC-TV program director, Connie Borge. Food stylist/producer Paul Diyorio is truly a bean's best friend. Registered dietician Suzanne Chasuk is always available with great tips and information.

Super-publicists Edna Farley and Lowell Farley have always been there for me with first-class advice. Also, Bernice Everett, Dottie Fretz, Richard Hack, Shelley Herman, Donald Sanders, and Ahrgus Julliard. Jim Melban of the California Dry Bean Advisory Board was very helpful, as was Dale Kuenzli, executive director of the Michigan Bean Commission.

I would also like to acknowledge Jeffrey Quaglino, who is missed a lot. And my first Roller Derby coaches Buddy Atkinson, Sr., and Bobbie Johnstone, who, back in 1972, knew I had a future in beans.

Finally, I'd like to thank Regis Philbin. Without Regis, I would never have written this book, nor have accomplished the things I've been proud of. Thank you, Regis. You're a wonderful guy! Joy's okay, too.

Contents

Introduction "It's Bean Time!"

Hey there! Thanks for picking up my book! And welcome to my wonderful world of beans. Whether you're an old hand at bean cuisine or a rookie, I guarantee you'll find my recipes to be the tastiest and classiest in all of beandom. And best of all, they're easy to make!

There is so much more to beans than heating and serving them out of a can. Beans are versatile! They make tempting appetizers, great-tasting main courses, and delicious desserts. And if that isn't enough, beans are healthful and relatively inexpensive! They can really help to stretch your food dollar. "Investment Cooking" . . . that's what I call it!

Use this book and I'll show you how to turn an ordinary can or bag of beans into a mouthwatering gourmet meal. And you don't have to search all over for fancy ingredients to do it. I use real ingredients for real people. If they're not in your pantry or refrigerator, they're as close as your corner market.

Beans . . . The Near-Perfect Food

We all know about the Seven Natural Wonders of the World, the Pyramids, the Grand Canyon, and so on. But there should have been an eighth, the lowly bean. Believe it or not, beans have been with us since 7000 B.C. Ancient civilizations believed beans held magical powers and could even ward off evil spirits! But most important, the riches beans possess are as astounding and amazing as the other wonders of the world.

The edible seeds of legume (pod-bearing) plants, beans have been called the near-perfect food because they are packed with protein, complex carbohydrates, B vitamins, iron, potassium, and magnesium. They contain very little fat and few calories. Beans are low in sodium, high in soluble fiber, and cholesterol-free. They even make us feel full, so we eat less and lose weight. Beans have become the rage not only because they taste great, but also because the government has issued dietary guidelines stating we should be eating more beans. Suddenly the humble bean has been thrust center stage and we are now taking a closer look at our diets . . . and the bean!

Beans of Plenty

There are more than 70 varieties of beans, many with names you have never heard of, such as, appaloosa, scarlet emperor, and Jacob's cattle. That's because they're hard to find. Most are stocked only in a few specialty stores and some health food stores. In this book I use 16 varieties of legumes that are readily available at your grocery store. But if you dare to be daring, feel free to experiment using "designer" beans in my recipes. Let's see . . . there are 75 recipes in my book × 70 beans = 5,200 recipes!

Gas . . . The Curse!

O.K. We all know that beans give us gas. Don't let it frighten you . . . it's natural. You see, there are certain complex sugars that beans possess that our small intestines just can't handle; thus, gas, or to put it more nicely, flatulence. The only sure way to get rid of gas is to eat beans regularly so that your system will get used to them. Quite frankly, I'm single, I live alone, I don't care!

Getting Started . . . Bean Prep

With a few exceptions my recipes begin with *cooked* beans. If you're a type A personality like me, feel free to use canned beans. They're much more convenient than cooking dry beans because they save time. The canning process has already "cooked" them! However, if you have all the time in the world and nothing better to do, you may start with dry beans.

Now, what I'm about to tell you is very revolutionary and may cause rioting in the streets, but despite what you've heard, it's not necessary to soak your beans! Ancient mythology and popular belief has it that soaking dry beans before cooking them can improve the flavor and texture of the beans, can get rid of the little "buggers" that cause gas, and can save lots of cooking time. Wrong! Soaking does absolutely nothing to improve the flavor or texture of the beans, and it is powerless to get rid of the "gas-causing monsters." Also, the cooking time it saves is minimal.

Forget Soaking and Start Cooking!

Simply pick through the dry beans you are going to use. Throw out any stones or other impurities . . . yick! Rinse the beans and place them in a pot with three times as much water as beans, about 6 cups of water for every pound of beans. Bring the beans to a rapid boil for about 2 minutes, then cover and simmer until tender. During this cooking process, the beans use the water to rehydrate. If the water level gets too low, add some more to make sure the beans are always covered and don't get "thirsty." Cooking times range from 40 minutes to several hours. So sit back and watch a couple of "soaps," as I do!

Fava beans and garbanzo beans take the longest to cook, usually 2 to 3 hours. Pinto beans, black beans, cannellini beans, Great Northern beans, navy beans, small white beans, butter beans, baby lima beans, kidney beans, pink beans, red beans, and pinquito beans usually take around 1 ½ to 2 hours to cook. Black-eyed peas and lentils take around 40 minutes to 1 hour to cook. These are only approximate cooking times. Accurate cooking times vary, depending not only on the variety and size of the beans but also on the age of the beans, altitude, and hardness of water.

Pressure Cooking

You may use a pressure cooker if you like. Place your dry beans in the cooker, pour in enough water to cover them, and add a tablespoon of vegetable oil or butter to prevent the beans from foaming and clogging the vent. Do not fill the cooker more than a third full of total ingredients: beans, water, and oil or butter. Cover and cook the beans at 15 pounds pressure for about 25 minutes for most beans. Garbanzos take about 35 minutes and favas around 45 minutes. Lentils take about 11 minutes, and black-eyed peas take even less, just 10 minutes. When finished cooking, reduce the pressure by running cold water over the lid. Or if you prefer, you can just remove the cooker from the heat to allow the pressure to gradually reduce. If you use this method, keep in mind that the beans will continue cooking, so you'll want to cut the cooking time by 2 or 3 minutes.

Bean Counting

I flunked arithmetic, but this much I'm sure about. To make the math simple for you, a 1-pound bag of dry beans = 2 cups *dry* or 5 to 6 cups *cooked* beans. One 15-ounce can, drained = almost 1 ½ cups *cooked* beans.

Bean Storage

Your leftover or unused cooked beans can last about four days in the refrigerator. You can also store them in sandwich bags in the freezer for up to a year. But why would you? You're on your way to becoming a bean lover. Bean lovers don't store . . . we eat!

Once you've prepared your beans, either by using a can opener or sweating over the stove, you're ready to make BEAN MAGIC! So click your heels together three times and repeat, "There's no food like beans, there's no food like beans, there's no food like beans!"

CHAPTER ONE

"Ready, Set, Go!" Soups and Starters

Just as a baby must learn to crawl before it can walk, an adult must learn to whet the appetite before taking the big dive into Main Course Nirvana! And what better way to whet the appetite than with my scrumptious bean appetizers.

Nothing warms those cold winter nights like a warm bowl of bean soup. My Black-eyed Yam Soup is the perfect starter on those cold, cold nights. The flavors of the savory black-eyed peas and sweet-tasting yams combine to tease your taste buds. Or how about my Black and

Pinto Bean Soup? Laced with more than a hint of sherry, it's sure to become a favorite!

Of course you'll want to try my zesty dips, which go perfectly on crackers, or with all kinds of sliced raw vegetables. While the dips you buy at the store are full of fat and lard, my dips are virtually fat-free. And best of all, you can whip up a batch in minutes. Try my Pinto Bean Dip, or my nephew's favorite, Nick's Favorite Black Bean Dip. They're perfect for any party or snack. In fact, they're a great excuse to throw a party! And don't forget . . . beans are international! I came up with the idea for Black Bean Potstickers because I love Chinese food and wanted a tasty appetizer to go along with my chow mein. Astounding Pinto Nachos complement any Mexican dish. Just remember to save room for your bean burrito!

Enjoy these and other exciting bean starters and I guarantee you'll be hooked on beans for life!

PintoBeanDip

Don't reach for that supermarket bean dip! It's full of fat and hydrogenated oils. Instead, whip up a batch of my fat-free Pinto Bean Dip. The mellow flavor of the beans is accentuated with the distinctive flavor of fresh lime juice.

Makes about 2 cups

INGREDIENTS

3 cups cooked pinto beans, drained, or 2 (15-ounce) cans pinto beans, drained and rinsed

2 tablespoons finely chopped green onion

1 clove garlic, finely chopped

½ teaspoon chopped fresh dill

3 tablespoons freshly squeezed lime juice

2 tablespoons seasoned rice vinegar

2 drops Tabasco sauce

METHOD

In a large bowl, mash beans until smooth. Add remaining ingredients and blend thoroughly.

Dive in!

Nick's Favorite Black Bean Dip

Where does a person get a love for beans? As far as I'm concerned, it all has to do with genetics. I realized this early on when I discovered that my nephew, Nick, would eat only black beans! And guess what? His favorite black bean recipe is the one that bears his name—Nick's Favorite Black Bean Dip. I hope this zesty recipe of hearty black beans and fresh herbs becomes a favorite of yours too.

Makes about 2 cups

INGREDIENTS

3 cups cooked black beans, drained, or 2 (15-ounce) cans black beans, drained and rinsed

2 tablespoons finely chopped green onion

1 clove garlic, minced

1 tablespoon chopped fresh cilantro

½ teaspoon chopped fresh dill

3 tablespoons freshly squeezed lime juice

2 tablespoons seasoned rice vinegar

¼ teaspoon cayenne pepper

M E T H O D

In a blender or food processor, puree beans.

In a large bowl, combine all ingredients and mix thoroughly.

Refrigerate for a couple of hours, and serve chilled.

BlueRibbon GarbanzoDip

I've finally liberated the garbanzo bean! What was once thought of only as garnish on top of a salad has evolved into a fabulous dip. These nutty-flavored garbanzos, mashed with zesty ingredients that include lemon juice and chili powder, make a terrific dip that takes only minutes to prepare. Although this dip hasn't really won any blue ribbons, it's number one in my book!

Makes about 2 cups

INGREDIENTS

3 cups cooked garbanzo beans, drained, or 2 (15-ounce) cans garbanzo beans, drained and rinsed

2 tablespoons freshly squeezed lemon juice

2 tablespoons seasoned rice vinegar

½ teaspoon chili powder

1 tablespoon chopped fresh cilantro

1 teaspoon extra-virgin olive oil

½ cup finely chopped red onion

1 clove garlic, minced

M E T H O D

In a large bowl, mash beans. Add lemon juice, rice vinegar, chili powder, and cilantro and mix well.

In a small skillet, heat olive oil over medium heat. Add onion and garlic and cook until garlic begins to brown. Transfer mixture to bowl and mix well.

Serve warm or chilled.

GreatNorthern BlackBeanDip

Mild-tasting Great Northerns and creamy black beans mashed together with sautéed fresh herbs and red onion make this dip a very flavorful treat, especially when seasoned with a little rice vinegar and hot Tabasco sauce! It's also a great way to get your children to cook because it's easy and a lot of fun. Simply place everything in a storage bag and mash!   **Makes about 2 cups**

I N G R E D I E N T S

1 cup cooked Great Northern beans, drained, or 1 cup canned Great Northern beans, drained and rinsed

1 cup cooked black beans, drained, or 1 cup canned black beans, drained and rinsed

1 tablespoon seasoned rice vinegar

2 drops Tabasco sauce

¼ teaspoon chopped fresh dill

1 tablespoon extra-virgin olive oil

¼ cup chopped red onion

¼ cup chopped fresh parsley

2 to 3 cloves garlic, minced

Dump beans into a large zip-type plastic storage bag. Make sure all air is out of bag. Seal. With a wooden mallet, mash beans to a paste.

Open storage bag. Add rice vinegar, Tabasco, and dill. Seal bag again and massage to mix everything up.

In a medium skillet, heat olive oil over medium heat. Add red onion, parsley, and garlic. Sauté for 2 minutes, then transfer to bag. Seal and massage again. With scissors, snip a corner of bag and squeeze mixture into a serving bowl.

Dip with crackers and all kinds of vegetables.

Cheesy Navy Bean Chowder

The U.S. Senate serves bean soup every day in their dining room, and now you can serve my Cheesy Navy Bean Chowder every day in *your* dining room! Cheddar cheese and Monterey Jack melted into a base of chicken broth make this soup especially flavorful. **Serves 6 to 8**

I N G R E D I E N T S

3 cups cooked navy beans, drained, or 2 (15-ounce) cans navy beans, drained and rinsed

3½ cups chicken broth

¾ cup shredded carrot

¾ cup shredded celery

1 small onion, shredded

1 (17-ounce) can whole-kernel corn, drained and pureed

½ teaspoon curry powder

¼ teaspoon garlic powder

½ cup shredded reduced-fat Monterey Jack cheese

½ cup shredded reduced-fat Cheddar cheese

M E T H O D

In a blender or food processor, puree 1½ cups navy beans.

Transfer pureed beans to a 3-quart saucepan. Add remaining beans, chicken broth, carrot, celery, and onion. Stir and bring to a boil.

Reduce heat. Stir in pureed corn, curry powder, and garlic powder and simmer 20 minutes, stirring occasionally. Remove from heat and stir in cheeses.

Serve immediately.

Black and Pinto Bean Soup

They say nothing hits the spot like Mom's homemade chicken soup. Well, that was before my hearty Black and Pinto Bean Soup came on the scene. The sherry I use hits the spot like Mom's chicken soup never could.   **Serves 4**

I N G R E D I E N T S

3 cups cooked black beans, drained, or 2 (15-ounce) cans black beans, drained and rinsed

1½ cups cooked pinto beans, drained, or 1 (15-ounce) can pinto beans, drained and rinsed

1 tablespoon vegetable oil

1 medium red onion, chopped

1 clove garlic, finely chopped

1 cup water

¾ cup cooking sherry

¼ cup freshly squeezed lime juice

¼ cup seasoned rice vinegar

¼ teaspoon black pepper

¼ teaspoon garlic powder

In a blender or food processor, puree ½ cup each of black beans and pinto beans.

In a large saucepan, heat vegetable oil over medium heat. Add onion and garlic and sauté until onion is tender.

Add water, sherry, and pureed and whole beans. Stir well and bring to a boil. Reduce heat and simmer 6 minutes, stirring occasionally.

Remove from heat and stir in lime juice, rice vinegar, black pepper, and garlic powder.

Serve immediately.

Heavenly
LentilSoup

I feel I must pay homage to the small lentil. While not technically a bean, the lentil is the oldest cultivated legume known to man. In fact, ancient Egyptian kings believed lentils held many powers. Well, I don't know about that, but I do know they make a wonderfully flavorful soup in a base of red wine, balsamic vinegar, fresh vegetables, and Monterey Jack cheese.   **Serves 4 to 6**

I N G R E D I E N T S

2 cups dry lentils, rinsed and drained

7 cups water

½ cup dry red wine

2 tablespoons balsamic vinegar

1 tablespoon extra-virgin olive oil

1 small potato, chopped

1 stalk celery, chopped

2 carrots, chopped

½ teaspoon garlic powder

1 cup shredded Monterey Jack cheese

M E T H O D

In a large pot, combine lentils, water, wine, vinegar, and olive oil and bring to a boil. Reduce heat. Add remaining ingredients except cheese and simmer until lentils are tender, about 40 minutes. Remove from heat and stir in cheese.

Serve immediately. I especially like to serve this soup with fresh sourdough French bread.

Hearty MinestroneSoup

When it comes to comfort food, nothing tops the list like Hearty Minestrone Soup. It's delicious and full of my favorite vegetables and two of my favorite beans: nutty garbanzos and robust dark red kidneys. An entire meal all by itself!

Serves 8

I N G R E D I E N T S

1 tablespoon extra-virgin olive oil

1 cup chopped onion

1 cup chopped celery

5½ cups chicken broth

1 (14½-ounce) can diced tomatoes, undrained

1 cup shell pasta

¼ teaspoon garlic powder

¼ teaspoon black pepper

½ teaspoon dried thyme

1 (16-ounce) can mixed vegetables, drained

1½ cups cooked dark red kidney beans, drained, or 1 (15-ounce) can dark red kidney beans, drained and rinsed

1½ cups cooked garbanzo beans, drained, or 1 (15-ounce) can garbanzo beans, drained and rinsed

M E T H O D

In a large pot, heat olive oil over medium heat. Add onion and celery and sauté until onion is tender.

Stir in chicken broth and diced tomatoes and bring to a boil.

Add shell pasta, garlic powder, black pepper, and thyme and stir to combine. Reduce heat, add mixed vegetables and beans, and simmer 10 to 15 minutes.

Serve immediately.

Black-eyed YamSoup

I developed this recipe while taking a nap. When I woke up, I immediately wrote it down, raced to the kitchen, and *presto!* . . . the best Black-eyed Yam Soup ever to hit my stomach. The flavors of savory black-eyed peas and sweet yams unite for a strikingly delectable delight!   **Serves 6**

I   N   G   R   E   D   I   E   N   T   S

1 ½ cups cooked black-eyed peas, drained, or
1 (15-ounce) can black-eyed peas, drained and rinsed

1 (16-ounce) can cut yams, drained and pureed

1 (8¾-ounce) can whole-kernel corn, drained

3½ cups chicken broth

¼ teaspoon garlic powder

¼ teaspoon black pepper

M   E   T   H   O   D

In a 3-quart saucepan, combine all ingredients. Stir and bring to a boil. Reduce heat and simmer 15 minutes.

Serve immediately.

Kidney Bean Soup

Kidney Bean Soup is a result of my failed attempt at inventing a quick recipe for red beans and rice. I'm so glad I stumbled onto it! I like my soup hot and spicy, but if you prefer a milder version, just cut down on the cayenne pepper.

Serves 5 to 6

I N G R E D I E N T S

3 cups cooked dark red kidney beans, drained, or 2 (15-ounce) cans dark red kidney beans, drained and rinsed

3½ cups chicken broth

2 cups chopped onion

½ cup chopped celery

1 tablespoon minced garlic

1 teaspoon dried thyme

½ teaspoon cayenne pepper

M E T H O D

In a blender or food processor, puree 1 cup of beans. Transfer to a 3-quart saucepan.

Add remaining ingredients. Stir and bring to a boil. Reduce heat and simmer 20 minutes.

Serve immediately.

Garlic Bean Bread

Pacify your hunger with a big hunk of Garlic Bean Bread. As you bite in, you'll notice a pleasant surprise—a hint of garlic! Goes great with soup and salad.   **Makes 1 loaf**

I N G R E D I E N T S

2 cups all-purpose flour

2 teaspoons baking powder

1 teaspoon garlic powder

¼ teaspoon baking soda

¼ teaspoon salt

¼ cup granulated sugar

3 large egg whites

½ cup brown sugar

1 ½ cups cooked pinto beans, drained and pureed, or 1 (15-ounce) can pinto beans, drained, rinsed, and pureed

⅓ cup butter, melted and cooled

Preheat oven to 350°F and grease a 4½ × 8½-inch loaf pan.

In a large bowl, combine flour, baking powder, garlic powder, baking soda, salt, and granulated sugar.

In a medium bowl, beat together egg whites, brown sugar, beans, and butter. Transfer bean mixture to flour mixture and stir until dry ingredients are moistened.

Transfer mixture to greased pan and bake until loaf is well browned, 50 to 55 minutes.

Cool in pan for 15 minutes; remove bread from pan and finish cooling on a wire rack.

Serve warm.

Bean Quesadillas

When I sit down to have a beer, I have to have a couple of Bean Quesadillas to go with it. They take only minutes to prepare, and the cilantro gives them a nice bite—or maybe it's the beer! For a change of pace and color, substitute red beans for small white beans.

Serves 4

I N G R E D I E N T S

1 ½ cups cooked small white beans or red beans, drained, or 1 (15-ounce) can small white beans or red beans, drained and rinsed

1 cup shredded Monterey Jack cheese

1 green onion, finely chopped

1 teaspoon finely chopped fresh cilantro

½ teaspoon garlic powder

4 large flour tortillas

M E T H O D

In a large bowl, lightly mash beans. Stir in cheese, green onion, cilantro, and garlic powder.

Divide mixture into fourths and spread a portion on each tortilla. Fold each tortilla in half.

Place 2 tortillas in a medium nonstick skillet over medium heat. Cook for about 2 minutes on each side, or until tortillas are golden brown and cheese has melted. Repeat with remaining 2 tortillas.

Slice quesadillas into thirds. Serve immediately, with a frosty glass of beer.

BlackBean
Potstickers

Potstickers come to us from northern China. But Black Bean
Potstickers can come only from your kitchen. Each potsticker
is packed with black beans, finely chopped fresh vegetables,
aromatic ginger, and cilantro and seasoned with soy sauce,
sesame oil, seasoned rice vinegar, and sherry.

Makes about 22 potstickers

I N G R E D I E N T S

1½ cups cooked black beans, drained, or 1 (15-ounce)
can black beans, drained and rinsed

¼ cup finely chopped green onion

¼ cup finely chopped carrot

¼ cup finely chopped water chestnuts

½ teaspoon minced fresh ginger

1 tablespoon soy sauce

2 teaspoons sesame oil

2 teaspoons seasoned rice vinegar

1 teaspoon sherry

1 teaspoon chopped fresh cilantro

22 potsticker skins or wonton wrappers

Vegetable oil

½ cup water

M E T H O D

In a medium bowl, combine all ingredients except pot-sticker skins, vegetable oil, and water. Mix thoroughly.

Place 1 tablespoon of mixture across the center of each potsticker skin and lightly moisten entire edge with some water. Seal edges together over mixture by pinching them to form a seam.

Cover bottom of medium nonstick skillet with vegetable oil. Add half of the potstickers, seam side up, and brown their bottoms over medium-high heat. Add ¼ cup water and immediately cover. Reduce heat to medium and cook for about 6 minutes.

When water is almost absorbed, uncover, increase heat to medium-high, and let remaining water boil away.

Transfer to a serving dish and repeat the process with remaining uncooked potstickers.

Serve warm, with your favorite dipping sauce. Or try a sauce of equal parts rice vinegar and soy sauce.

Kidney Bean Salad Dressing

The hearty flavor of kidney beans together with sour cream and a hint of basil and garlic makes for a tangy, sweet dressing that takes only seconds to make in your blender! Wonderful over fresh spinach leaves. **Makes 2 cups**

I N G R E D I E N T S

1 ½ cups cooked dark red kidney beans, drained, or 1 (15-ounce) can dark red kidney beans, drained and rinsed

16 ounces reduced-fat sour cream

1 clove garlic

1 tablespoon chopped fresh basil

M E T H O D

In a blender, combine all ingredients and puree.

Serve over fresh spinach leaves.

KidneyBeanSalsa

This refreshing, zesty salsa is a great way to start a meal . . . and conversation. It takes only minutes to make, but your guests won't stop talking about it for days! If you like your salsa hot, add a chopped jalapeño pepper.

Makes approximately 4 cups

I N G R E D I E N T S

3 cups cooked dark red kidney beans, drained and chopped, or 2 (15-ounce) cans dark red kidney beans, drained, rinsed, and chopped

1 yellow or red onion, minced

1 (14½-ounce) can diced tomatoes, undrained

1 (4-ounce) can minced green chiles

1 small jalapeño pepper, minced (optional)

¼ teaspoon garlic powder

1 tablespoon freshly squeezed lime juice

1 tablespoon seasoned rice vinegar

M E T H O D

In a large bowl, combine all ingredients and mix well.

Dip into salsa with fat-free chips you can make yourself by cutting corn tortillas into triangles and baking.

Astounding PintoNachos

This is the perfect appetizer—it feeds lots of guests, but takes only minutes to prepare! This recipe contains just 5 ingredients and takes less than 10 minutes from start to finish. My Astounding Pinto Nachos are so good, you may never get to the main course. You'll love the flavorful combination of pinto beans, jalapeño peppers, green onions, and Cheddar cheese.

Serves 8

INGREDIENTS

1 (14-ounce) package corn tortilla strips

1½ cups cooked pinto beans, drained, or 1 (15-ounce) can pinto beans, drained and rinsed

3 medium jalapeño peppers, finely chopped

½ cup chopped green onion

2½ cups shredded Cheddar cheese

M E T H O D

Preheat oven to 400°F.

Place tortilla strips on 2 baking sheets. Spread beans on top of strips. Sprinkle with peppers and green onion and top with cheese.

Bake 5 minutes, or until cheese melts.

Serve immediately.

CHAPTER TWO

"The Early Bird Catches the Bean"

Breakfast, Brunch, and Lunch

They say that breakfast is the most important meal of the day. I agree! So every morning I pop out of bed, bright and chipper, at 5:00 A.M. and head straight for the kitchen to prepare a bean breakfast that's full of protein, carbohydrates, and vitamins.

Instead of plain old scrambled eggs, I fix myself a plate of Scrambled Olive Eggs à la Garbanzo. It's so good! The eggs are blended with tasty, colorful green olives, Cheddar cheese, and nutty-flavored garbanzos. Yum yum!

Of course, some mornings when I'm in a hurry, I just drink a glass of my Banana Bean Delight Energy Shake. I concocted this recipe when I realized I could save time by putting some of my favorite breakfast foods together in a blender! All I do is blend fresh orange juice with mild-tasting Great Northern beans, some nonfat yogurt, and a banana. Presto! An entire meal in a glass. It's everything I need to get that energy boost that lasts through the day.

The day doesn't end with my bean breakfast. I have a little bean brunch, and a little bean lunch too! By the way, I think brunch is the same as breakfast or lunch except you drink champagne instead of milk.

And nothing goes better with my champagne brunch than a serving of Fried Bananas and Kidneys. It's hard to describe the flavor, but I love the aroma and taste of banana slices sizzling with robust, sweet red kidney beans. Try this elegant, delicious recipe over waffles and pancakes.

For lunch I like things simple and easy. That's why I love peanut butter sandwiches! Unfortunately peanut butter is too fattening, so I had to invent Bean Peanut Spread. By simply blending mashed white beans with peanut butter, I cut the fat by almost 100 percent! Best of all, it still tastes like peanut butter.

I know you're going to love these and my other breathtaking recipes in this chapter, but remember to save room for dinner!

Kidney Bean Pancakes

When I wake up in the morning, the first thing I do is say a little prayer and have a little beans. Pancakes by themselves contain very little protein, but when you add chopped dark red kidney beans to the batter, you add not only protein and fiber but an incredible, indescribable flavor!

Makes 7 to 8 pancakes

INGREDIENTS

1 cup "just add water" buttermilk pancake mix
(I prefer Krusteaz)

¾ cup water

½ cup cooked dark red kidney beans, drained and chopped, or ½ cup canned dark red kidney beans, drained, rinsed, and chopped

METHOD

In a large bowl, combine all ingredients and mix well.

On a hot skillet, pour ¼ cup batter for each pancake. When pancakes bubble and bottoms are golden, flip once in mid-air.

Serve pancakes that survive with warmed maple syrup.

Scrambled Olive Eggs à la Garbanzo

Back in the '50s when I was a mere tot, my daddy sat me on the stove (it was off) and prepared the most delicious breakfast I had ever had since strained bananas. His creation . . . olive eggs. Just two weeks ago, I sat my dad on the stove and prepared his favorite breakfast with a twist, Scrambled Olive Eggs à la Garbanzo! Using only 4 ingredients—eggs, garbanzo beans, Cheddar cheese, and green olives—this recipe is a snap!   **Serves 2**

I N G R E D I E N T S

4 large eggs or 1 (8-ounce) carton egg substitute

½ cup cooked garbanzo beans, drained, or ½ cup canned garbanzo beans, drained and rinsed

½ cup shredded reduced-fat Cheddar cheese

10 pitted green olives

M E T H O D

In a blender, combine all ingredients and blend thoroughly.

Pour mixture into a nonstick skillet and scramble over medium-high heat until eggs are firm.

Serve immediately.

Stuffed
Black-eyed Omelet

Black-eyes are very common in Southern dishes, but they're also very versatile and should be used more in breakfast cuisine, such as my Stuffed Black-eyed Omelet. The filling of black-eyes, Cheddar cheese, and minced fresh parsley is to die for! **Makes 1 omelet**

I N G R E D I E N T S

3 large eggs

1 tablespoon water

Pinch of black pepper

1 tablespoon butter

3 tablespoons cooked black-eyed peas, drained,
or 3 tablespoons canned black-eyed peas,
drained and rinsed

1 tablespoon shredded Cheddar cheese

1 teaspoon minced fresh parsley

M E T H O D

In a small bowl, mix eggs, water, and pepper with a fork until well blended.

In an 8-inch omelet pan, heat butter over medium heat until it begins to sizzle. Add egg mixture.

As bottom of omelet begins to set, slide a spatula underneath and lift cooked portions of omelet so that the uncooked egg mixture flows underneath to the center. Cook until center and top are just moist, almost creamy.

Sprinkle filling of black-eyed peas, cheese, and parsley across center of omelet. Fold omelet in half.

Slide omelet gently onto a plate, and serve immediately.

Banana Bean Delight Energy Shake

You'll be ready to get up and face the world when you start the day with my great-tasting, refreshing Banana Bean Delight Energy Shake! It's got the wholesomeness of orange juice, the goodness of yogurt, and the fiber, carbohydrates, and protein of beans. **Makes 2 large glasses**

I N G R E D I E N T S

2 cups freshly squeezed orange juice

½ cup cooked Great Northern beans, drained, or ½ cup canned Great Northern beans, drained and rinsed

½ cup plain nonfat yogurt

1 banana

M E T H O D

In a blender, combine all ingredients and blend thoroughly.

Pour into tall glasses and serve.

BeanMuffins

Do you know the Muffin Man? Of course you do, but do you know about my delicious Bean Muffins? They're quick and easy to make. Just blend a few dark red kidney beans with some cream cheese and you've got a sweet, rich-tasting, colorful spread ready to top your toasted English muffins. It's also appetizing on bagels! **Makes 4 muffins**

I N G R E D I E N T S

4 English muffins, split

1 (8-ounce) package reduced-fat cream cheese

½ cup cooked dark red kidney beans, drained, or ½ cup canned dark red kidney beans, drained and rinsed

M E T H O D

In a blender or food processor, combine cream cheese and beans and blend thoroughly.

Toast muffins (8 halves).

Spread mixture on toasted muffins.

Serve with a tall glass of freshly squeezed orange juice.

BeanHash

Hash has always been a good way to use leftover meat. But instead of leftover meat, I use leftover black beans and large butter beans. When they are cooked with onion, potatoes, garlic powder, and pepper, you can't even tell that these beans were leftovers! **Serves 4**

I N G R E D I E N T S

1½ cups cooked large butter beans, drained and mashed, or 1 (15-ounce) can large butter beans, drained, rinsed, and mashed

1½ cups cooked black beans, drained and mashed, or 1 (15-ounce) can black beans, drained, rinsed, and mashed

1 small onion, finely chopped

2 cups chopped boiled potato

¼ teaspoon garlic powder

¼ teaspoon black pepper

1 tablespoon extra-virgin olive oil

In a large bowl, combine beans, onion, potato, garlic powder, and pepper and mix well.

In a medium skillet, heat olive oil over medium-high heat. Spread bean mixture evenly over bottom of skillet. Press down firmly on mixture with the back of a spatula. Cook for about 8 minutes, or until a crust forms on the bottom, then break up and stir crust into hash.

Press mixture firmly again and cook for about 8 minutes more.

Break up and serve immediately.

FriedBananas andKidneys

Now, I know this recipe sounds a bit unusual, and it is! Unusually good! The aroma of banana slices and dark red kidney beans sautéing in butter and brown sugar is overwhelming. Serve this elegant dish alone or as a topping on hot waffles.   **Serves 4**

I N G R E D I E N T S

2 tablespoons butter

1½ cups sliced banana

¼ cup brown sugar

1½ cups cooked dark red kidney beans, drained and mashed, or 1 (15-ounce) can dark red kidney beans, drained, rinsed, and mashed

M E T H O D

In a large skillet, melt butter over medium heat. Place banana slices on bottom of skillet and cook for about 1 minute.

Top banana slices with brown sugar, then flip banana slices.

Add beans and continue to flip bananas and beans together for about 1 minute, or until beans are warm.

Serve immediately.

Ham'n'Beans in Maple Syrup

Move over ham 'n' eggs! Meet the new kid on the block, Ham 'n' Beans in Maple Syrup! Maple syrup livens up the mild Great Northerns and brings out the flavor of the chopped smoked ham. Terrific with a tall glass of freshly squeezed orange juice or champagne.   **Serves 2**

I N G R E D I E N T S

1 ½ cups cooked Great Northern beans, drained, and patted dry, or 1 (15-ounce) can Great Northern beans, drained, rinsed, and patted dry

¼ cup maple syrup

⅓ cup chopped smoked ham

2 sprigs parsley

M E T H O D

In a small bowl, combine all ingredients and mix well.

Transfer to 2 small baking dishes and heat in a microwave oven or toaster oven on high for 1 minute.

Top with sprigs of parsley and serve immediately.

BlackBeans andSausage

I found breakfast sausage a little boring, so I decided to spice things up a bit; hence, Black Beans and Sausage. You guessed it. I've added earthy black beans, but there's also spicy chopped onion and red bell pepper for bright color and sweetness! **Serves 4**

I N G R E D I E N T S

1 tablespoon extra-virgin olive oil

1 small onion, chopped

⅔ cup diced red bell pepper

12 ounces pork sausage

1 ½ cups cooked black beans, drained, or 1 (15-ounce) can black beans, drained and rinsed

M E T H O D

In a large skillet, heat olive oil over medium heat. Add onion and bell pepper and sauté until tender.

Add sausage and cook thoroughly.

Add beans and cook until they are heated through.

Serve immediately.

Beans in a Blanket

This burrito is a cross between a morning burrito and an evening burrito. Meaty pinto beans, cottage cheese, mild-tasting Colby cheese, and green onions are all wrapped up in a flour tortilla. **Serves 4**

I N G R E D I E N T S

½ cup cottage cheese

⅓ cup shredded Colby cheese

¼ cup chopped green onion

1½ cups cooked pinto beans, drained, or 1 (15-ounce) can pinto beans, drained and rinsed

4 taco-size (8-inch) flour tortillas

M E T H O D

In a medium bowl, combine cottage cheese, Colby cheese, and green onion. Add beans and mix well.

Divide mixture into fourths and place a portion on top of each tortilla.

Fold tortillas in half and heat in a microwave oven on high for 1 minute.

Serve immediately.

Baked Bean Potato Skins

These skins are loaded with flavorful pinquito beans and enlivened with melted butter, colorful paprika, dill, and white pepper. I just love to serve my Baked Bean Potato Skins to guests while I'm barbecuing. It gives them something delicious to put in their mouths instead of whining about when the chicken's going to be done! By the way, if you can't find pinquito beans, use pink beans.

Makes 12 skins

I N G R E D I E N T S

6 medium baking potatoes

Extra-virgin olive oil

¼ cup butter

¼ teaspoon paprika

¼ teaspoon dillweed

Pinch of white pepper

1½ cups cooked pinquito beans or pink beans, drained, or 1 (15-ounce) can pinquito beans, drained and rinsed

¼ cup chopped chives

1 cup shredded Cheddar cheese

M E T H O D

Preheat oven to 400°F.

Scrub potatoes, pat dry, and rub with a little olive oil. Pierce each potato in several places with a fork.

Place potatoes on a baking sheet and bake 45 minutes to 1 hour, or until they are tender when pierced.

When cooled, slice potatoes in half lengthwise. Scoop out potato pulp, leaving each potato skin ⅛ inch thick. (Reserve the scooped-out potato pulp for Incredible Edible Mashed Bean Potatoes.) Return potato skins to baking sheet.

In a small pan, melt butter over low heat. Add paprika, dillweed, and white pepper. Brush inside of potato skins with mixture, add beans, and top with chives and cheese.

Bake until crispy, about 20 minutes.

Serve immediately.

Grilled Garbanzo and Cheese Sandwich

We all know how binding the classic grilled cheese sandwich can be. I've countered this problem by adding a healthy dose of fiber-filled garbanzos. Adding to the flavor of this scrumptious sandwich are thin slices of sweet and colorful red onion.

Makes 2 sandwiches

I N G R E D I E N T S

1 tablespoon butter

4 slices of sandwich bread, any kind

½ cup cooked garbanzo beans, drained and chopped, or ½ cup canned garbanzo beans, drained, rinsed, and chopped

2 thin slices red onion

⅔ cup shredded Cheddar cheese

M E T H O D

In a medium nonstick skillet, melt butter over medium heat.

Place 2 slices of bread in the skillet. Top each slice of bread, with half the beans and a slice of onion. Cover beans and onions with cheese. Place remaining bread slices on top of each sandwich.

Cover skillet and heat until most of cheese is melted and bottom of sandwich has browned. Flip each sandwich, re-cover, and heat 2 minutes more, or until bottoms have browned.

Serve immediately.

Bean Peanut Spread

Peanut butter is very fattening, but not my Bean Peanut Spread. One serving of reduced-fat peanut butter has approximately 12 grams of fat, but when it is augmented with a cup of mashed Great Northern beans, one serving transforms to barely more than 1 gram of fat (and you can make five times as many sandwiches too). Best of all, it tastes just like peanut butter. Now that's what I call a miracle!

Makes 5 sandwiches

I N G R E D I E N T S

1 cup cooked Great Northern beans, drained, or 1 cup canned Great Northern beans, drained and rinsed

2 tablespoons reduced-fat peanut butter

M E T H O D

In a small bowl, mash beans with a spoon until smooth. Add peanut butter and blend thoroughly.

Spread on sandwich bread, top with bananas or jelly, and serve!

White Bean Tuna Sandwiches

If you have a tough time getting your kids to eat their beans, my White Bean Tuna Sandwiches just might be the answer. When the beans are mashed and blended with ingredients such as onions, dill pickle, and lemon juice, those little rascals will never know they just tasted the wonderful magic of beans.   **Makes 4 sandwiches**

I N G R E D I E N T S

1 (6⅛-ounce) can white tuna, drained

2 tablespoons fat-free mayonnaise

½ cup cooked small white beans or navy beans, drained and mashed, or ½ cup canned small white beans or navy beans, drained, rinsed, and mashed

1 green onion, chopped

¼ cup finely chopped red onion

1 small dill pickle, finely chopped

1 tablespoon seasoned rice vinegar

2 tablespoons freshly squeezed lemon juice

M E T H O D

In a large bowl, combine all ingredients and mix well.

Spread on sandwich bread and enjoy.

CHAPTER THREE

"StarLight, StarBright, WhichBean Shall I Cook Tonight?" MainCourses

From the moment I awake, I daydream about what to make for dinner. Shall I make Pinto Patties? How about Bean Lasagna? Oh, I know. Bean Pizza! When it comes to the versatile bean, it's never an easy choice.

I love big, fat, juicy hamburgers, but from time to time I also enjoy my exquisite Pinto Patties. Not only are they as exciting as a big, fat, juicy hamburger, but they contain very little fat! Try mashing pinto beans together with sautéd chopped onion, parsley, and fresh herbs. Form into patties, then warm on a grill. They are a wonderful, refreshing change of pace.

When I'm in the mood for Italian food, I can serve up my tempting Bean Pizza in just 10 minutes! I simply take a can of tomato sauce, stir in some oregano, basil, and thyme, and pour over a bed of sautéd vegetables and delicious dark red kidney beans and garbanzo beans. Incredible! What could be simpler? Pintos and Pasta, of course! Angel hair pasta folded into a cheesy bean sauce.

Now and then I really like to spice things up with Curried String Beans. Steamed fresh string beans are at their best bubbling in curry sauce with chopped red bell pepper and onion. It's not only a delicious dish but a beautiful one as well.

Of course you'll want to try my favorite comfort food, Kidney Bean Turkey Loaf. Meaty dark red kidney beans mixed with a pound of ground turkey breast along with chopped onion, pasta sauce, and Dijon mustard are especially tempting. And if you're a baked bean fan, you'll want to try such delights as my savory Quick Boston Baked Beans and my spicy Black Bean Cuban Bake.

These are just a few of the great-tasting entrees from which to choose. The choices are difficult. Sometimes life just isn't fair.

Pintos and Pasta

Beans are a wonderful way to add protein to your favorite pasta dish. Not only that, Pintos and Pasta is a recipe that takes only 5 minutes to prepare but tastes so great your guest will think you spent hours in the kitchen! **Serves 2**

INGREDIENTS

1 cup tomato and basil pasta sauce

1 ½ cups cooked pinto beans, drained, or 1 (15-ounce) can pinto beans, drained and rinsed

½ cup shredded Cheddar cheese

4 ounces angel hair pasta, cooked al dente and drained

METHOD

In a 3-quart saucepan, combine pasta sauce and beans over medium heat, stirring occasionally until hot.

Add cheese and blend until cheese has melted. Add cooked pasta and fold gently.

Serve immediately with a bottle of wine.

PintoPatties

Hamburgers are an American staple, but they're full of fat and cholesterol. A healthy alternative is the herb-packed Pinto Patty. I first made the Pinto Patty on a television show with Linda Dano. Unfortunately for Linda, at the end of the segment she accidentally bit into an ice cold, uncooked one and hasn't been able to pick up a Pinto Patty since.

Makes 5 to 6 patties

I N G R E D I E N T S

3 cups cooked pinto beans, drained, or 2 (15-ounce) cans pinto beans, drained and rinsed

¾ cup bread crumbs

1 ounce seasoned rice vinegar

Pinch of Spike (all-purpose seasoning)

2 large egg whites

1 tablespoon extra-virgin olive oil

6 cloves garlic, chopped

¼ cup chopped fresh parsley

2 green onions, chopped

M E T H O D

In a large bowl, mash beans. Add bread crumbs, rice vinegar, Spike, and egg whites and mix well.

In a small skillet, heat olive oil over medium heat. Add garlic, parsley, and green onions and sauté until onions are tender. Transfer to bowl and blend thoroughly.

Form mixture into patties and cook on a preheated grill until patties are lightly browned and heated through.

Serve immediately.

BeanPizza

Pizza is one of the most popular dishes on earth. It's easy to make and nutritious. In this recipe I use kidney beans and garbanzo beans instead of sausage and cheese. You'll still have the texture, but without all the fat and cholesterol. The beans are showered with a simple, pleasing herb sauce for a wonderful flavor. You won't even miss the sausage and cheese.   **Serves 4 to 6**

I N G R E D I E N T S

1 (8-ounce) can tomato sauce

½ teaspoon dried oregano

½ teaspoon dried basil

½ teaspoon dried thyme

2 cloves garlic, minced

1 tablespoon seasoned rice vinegar

1 cup sliced vegetables, any kind (I like onions, bell peppers, and carrots)

1 (12-inch) ready-made heat-and-serve pizza crust

½ cup cooked dark red kidney beans, drained and chopped, or ½ cup canned dark red kidney beans, drained, rinsed, and chopped

½ cup cooked garbanzo beans, drained and chopped, or ½ cup canned garbanzo beans, drained, rinsed, and chopped

M E T H O D

Preheat oven to 450°F.

In a small bowl, combine tomato sauce, oregano, basil, thyme, and garlic.

In a skillet, heat rice vinegar. Add vegetables and sauté until tender.

Place pizza crust on a baking sheet or pizza pan and pour tomato sauce mixture on top. Spread vegetables over sauce and top with beans.

Bake 8 minutes, or until crust is crispy and tomato sauce bubbles.

Open wide!

Magnificent
PintoSurprise

Tasty pinto beans and ground turkey breast bathed in sautéd chopped onion and bubbling sour cream with chopped Roma tomatoes is a most luscious one-pan entree, especially when topped with Cheddar cheese.   **Serves 6**

I N G R E D I E N T S

1 tablespoon extra-virgin olive oil

1 small onion, chopped

1 pound ground turkey breast

1 ½ cups cooked pinto beans, drained, or 1 (15-ounce) can pinto beans, drained and rinsed

½ cup reduced-fat sour cream

3 Roma (plum) tomatoes, seeded and chopped

1 teaspoon black pepper

1 cup shredded Cheddar cheese

In a large skillet, heat olive oil over medium heat. Add onion and sauté until tender.

Add ground turkey and brown.

Add beans, sour cream, tomatoes, and pepper and simmer for several minutes, stirring occasionally.

Top with cheese. When cheese starts to melt, remove from heat.

Serve immediately.

Green Bean
Vegetable Medley
Casserole

Who says you can't get kids to eat canned green beans! Try this recipe and you'll have them eating green beans morning, noon, and night. This colorful cornucopia of French-style green beans and fresh vegetables makes for an enticing casserole you're sure to love. **Serves 4**

I N G R E D I E N T S

1 (15-ounce) can French-style green beans, drained

1 ½ cups chopped onion

1 medium red potato, diced

⅓ cup chopped fresh broccoli

⅓ cup chopped fresh cauliflower

1 cup shredded Cheddar cheese

M E T H O D

Preheat oven to 350°F.

In a 2-quart casserole, combine all vegetables and half of the cheese. Sprinkle remaining cheese on top and cover.

Bake 30 minutes.

Serve immediately.

Bean Lasagna

Sure, you *like* your lasagna recipe, but here's one you're sure to *love*. My Bean Lasagna tastes great! I substitute flavorful earthy black beans and nutty garbanzos for fatty ground beef.

Serves 8 to 10

INGREDIENTS

1 (8-ounce) package lasagna noodles

3 tablespoons butter

½ cup chopped celery

½ cup chopped onion

⅓ cup chopped red bell pepper

1 (28-ounce) can diced tomatoes with their juice

1 (6-ounce) can tomato paste

½ cup water

1 teaspoon dried basil

½ teaspoon sugar

½ teaspoon salt

¼ teaspoon black pepper

¼ teaspoon garlic powder

1 ½ cups cooked black beans, drained, or 1 (15-ounce) can black beans, drained and rinsed

1 ½ cups cooked garbanzo beans, drained, or 1 (15-ounce) can garbanzo beans, drained and rinsed

4 cups shredded mozzarella cheese

M E T H O D

Preheat oven to 350°F. Grease a 13 × 9-inch baking pan.

Cook lasagna noodles according to package directions.

Meanwhile, in a large saucepan, melt butter over medium heat. Add celery, onion, and bell pepper and sauté until tender. Stir in tomatoes, tomato paste, water, basil, sugar, salt, pepper, and garlic and bring to a boil. Reduce heat. Add beans and simmer 15 minutes.

In greased pan, layer 4 lasagna noodles on the bottom of the pan, followed by a layer of bean mixture, then a layer of cheese. Repeat this layering process two more times.

Bake 30 to 45 minutes, until lasagna is bubbly.

Let lasagna sit for 5 minutes, then serve hot.

Excellent!

MightyBean Burritos

Dark red kidney beans have a natural affinity for rice, which makes these burritos special in texture and flavor, especially when enriched with green onions, sliced garlic, and tomato sauce.

Makes 4 burritos

I N G R E D I E N T S

1½ cups cooked dark red kidney beans, drained, or 1 (15-ounce) can dark red kidney beans, drained and rinsed

1 (8¾-ounce) can whole-kernel corn, drained

3 green onions, chopped

3 cloves garlic, sliced

1 (15-ounce) can tomato sauce

2 cups cooked rice

4 large flour tortillas

You can use black beans

M E T H O D

In a large saucepan, combine all ingredients except rice and tortillas. Bring to a boil, reduce heat, and simmer 4 minutes, stirring occasionally.

Remove from heat and let sit, covered, 4 minutes. Stir in rice.

Spoon mixture down center of warm tortillas, fold sides over, and serve.

Quick Boston Baked Beans

Do you know why they call Boston "Bean Town"? It's because it's famous for Boston Baked Beans! Traditionally, this savory dish of navy beans, molasses, and other flavorful ingredients can take more than 3 hours to prepare, but I've taken care of that. My version takes no more than 45 minutes from oven to stomach! **Serves 4**

I N G R E D I E N T S

1 teaspoon extra-virgin olive oil

1 medium onion, chopped

3 cups cooked navy beans, drained, or 2 (15-ounce) cans navy beans, drained and rinsed

½ cup chopped cooked smoked ham (optional)

3 tablespoons molasses

¼ cup brown sugar

1 tablespoon dry mustard

¼ teaspoon garlic powder

M E T H O D

Preheat oven to 350°F.

In a medium skillet, heat olive oil over medium heat. Add onion and sauté until tender.

Transfer onion to a 2-quart casserole and add remaining ingredients. Mix well and cover.

Bake 45 minutes, stirring once after 20 minutes.

Serve immediately.

BeanBoats

This is the perfect way to eat a baked potato. Bean Boats are simply baked potato skins restuffed and rebaked with their potato pulp, which has been blended with dark red kidney beans, Cheddar cheese, red onion, and garlic. Yummy! **Makes 4 boats**

I N G R E D I E N T S

2 baking potatoes

Extra-virgin olive oil

2 tablespoons butter

½ cup shredded Cheddar cheese

¼ cup finely chopped red onion

2 cloves garlic, finely chopped

¾ cup cooked dark red kidney beans, drained and chopped, or ¾ cup canned dark red kidney beans, drained, rinsed, and chopped

½ teaspoon chopped fresh rosemary (optional)

M E T H O D

Preheat oven to 400°F.

Scrub potatoes, pat dry, and rub with a little olive oil. Pierce each potato in several places with a fork.

Place potatoes on a baking sheet and bake 45 minutes to 1 hour, or until they are tender when pierced.

When cooled, slice potatoes in half lengthwise. Scoop out potato pulp and place in a large bowl. (Save potato shells.) Blend in butter, ¼ cup cheese, onion, garlic, beans, and rosemary.

Place potato shells in a shallow baking pan and spoon mixture into shells. Top with remaining cheese and bake an additional 10 minutes.

Smile and eat!

White Christmas Chicken Chili

A real-life cowboy named Cowboy Mike took one whiff of my white bean chili and said, "My stars! This is definitely White Christmas Chili!" The name stuck. Great Northerns and Monterey Jack cheese combine to complement the ground chicken in flavor, texture, and color.

Serves 6 to 8

INGREDIENTS

1 teaspoon extra-virgin olive oil

1 pound ground chicken

1 large onion, chopped

1 quart chicken broth

3 cups cooked Great Northern beans, drained, or 2 (15-ounce) cans Great Northern beans, drained and rinsed

1 (4-ounce) can chopped green chiles

½ cup chopped red bell pepper

1 teaspoon dried oregano

1 teaspoon ground cumin

¼ teaspoon garlic powder

Pinch of cayenne pepper

1 cup shredded Monterey Jack cheese

In a large skillet, heat olive oil over medium heat. Add chicken and onion and sauté until chicken is thoroughly cooked.

Transfer mixture to a 3-quart saucepan. Stir in chicken broth, beans, chiles, bell pepper, oregano, cumin, garlic powder, and cayenne pepper and bring to a boil. Reduce heat and simmer 10 minutes.

Remove from heat and stir in cheese.

Serve immediately, and savor while waiting for Santa.

Baked Black-eyes and Ham

The aroma that surrounds your kitchen while baking this recipe is enough to make you want to cook Baked Black-eyes and Ham every night of the week! The secret to this successful recipe is the distinctively strong flavor of Dijon mustard. **Serves 4**

I N G R E D I E N T S

1 tablespoon extra-virgin olive oil

1 cup diced onion

3 cups cooked black-eyed peas, drained, or 2 (15-ounce) cans black-eyed peas, drained and rinsed

1 cup diced cooked smoked ham

½ teaspoon garlic powder

1 tablespoon Dijon mustard

2 tablespoons seasoned rice vinegar

½ cup brown sugar

M E T H O D

Preheat oven to 325°F.

In a small skillet, heat olive oil over medium heat. Add onion and sauté until tender.

Transfer sautéd onion to a 2-quart casserole. Add remaining ingredients and mix gently.

Bake, uncovered, 45 minutes, stirring once after 20 minutes.

Serve immediately.

Bean-Stuffed Bell Peppers

There's more than one way to stuff a bell pepper. If you can stuff it with ground beef, you can stuff it with heavenly, mellow pinto beans along with other flavor-enhancing ingredients such as onion, garlic, and Parmesan cheese.

Makes 6 medium stuffed bell peppers

I N G R E D I E N T S

6 medium bell peppers

1 tablespoon extra-virgin olive oil

¼ cup chopped onion

1 clove garlic, minced

1 (8-ounce) can tomato sauce

1½ cups cooked pinto beans, drained, or 1 (15-ounce) can pinto beans, drained and rinsed

1 cup cooked rice

1 (8¾-ounce) can whole-kernel corn, drained

½ teaspoon chopped fresh dill

Pinch of black pepper

3 tablespoons freshly shredded Parmesan cheese

2 tablespoons chopped fresh parsley

Preheat oven to 350°F. Bring a large pot of water to a boil.

Cut tops off peppers and remove seeds. Immerse peppers in boiling water and cook for about 10 minutes. Remove and turn upside down to drain.

In a large skillet, heat olive oil over medium heat. Add onion and garlic and sauté until onion is tender. Blend in tomato sauce, beans, rice, corn, dill, and pepper and cook until heated through.

Place peppers in a large baking dish and stuff with bean mixture. Top with cheese and parsley.

Bake, uncovered, 15 minutes.

Serve immediately.

BlackBean
TurkeyTacos

I love Mexican food, and although the pinto bean is the bean that is often associated with it, I love black beans in Mexican food. What I like most about beans is that they're interchangeable in almost any recipe. To cut down on fat, I use ground turkey breast. The flavor of the turkey blended with the black beans makes this an especially mouthwatering treat. Enjoy.   **Makes 12 tacos**

I   N   G   R   E   D   I   E   N   T   S

1 pound ground turkey breast

⅔ cup chopped red onion

1½ cups cooked black beans, drained and chopped, or 1
(15-ounce) can black beans, drained, rinsed, and
chopped

1 (8¾-ounce) can whole-kernel corn, drained

12 corn tortillas

5 Roma (plum) tomatoes, chopped

2 green onions, chopped

1 tablespoon chopped fresh cilantro

M E T H O D

In a large nonstick skillet over medium-high heat, sauté ground turkey with red onion until turkey is thoroughly cooked.

Add beans and corn and cook, stirring constantly, for 2 minutes.

Spoon a portion of turkey mixture down center of each tortilla and fold sides over.

Top with tomatoes, green onions, and cilantro and serve with a smile.

Curried
String Beans

There's nothing quite as tasty as string beans bathed in curry, which is actually a combination of several spices: cumin, black mustard seed, coriander, fenugreek, and turmeric. This is not only a delicious way to eat string beans but a beautiful dish too. **Serves 6**

I N G R E D I E N T S

3 tablespoons extra-virgin olive oil

1 medium onion, diced

2 cloves garlic, minced

⅓ cup diced red bell pepper

1 jalapeño pepper, minced

2 tablespoons mild curry powder

¼ cup flour

2 cups chicken broth

1 pound fresh string beans, steamed

In a large skillet, heat olive oil over medium heat. Add onion and garlic and sauté until onion is tender.

Stir in bell pepper, jalapeño pepper, curry powder, flour, and chicken broth. Add string beans and cook for 5 to 10 minutes, or until heated through.

Serve immediately.

Baked Butter Beans with Hot Dogs

Large butter beans really do have a creamy, buttery flavor and are especially delectable when combined with sautéd onion rings, hot dogs, and melted Cheddar cheese. This is my favorite way to eat hot dogs, but to cut down on fat, I use reduced-fat brands. **Serves 4**

I N G R E D I E N T S

3 cups cooked large butter beans, drained, or 2 (15-ounce) cans large butter beans, drained and rinsed

1 tablespoon extra-virgin olive oil

1 medium onion, sliced into thin rings and separated

2 hot dogs, chopped into small bits

¾ cup shredded Cheddar cheese

M E T H O D

Preheat oven to 325°F.

Place beans in a 2-quart casserole.

In a small skillet, heat olive oil over medium heat. Add onion rings and sauté until tender.

Spread sautéd onions evenly over beans. Scatter hot dog bits evenly over onions. Sprinkle cheese evenly over hot dog bits.

Cover and bake 40 minutes.

Serve immediately.

Bean Stew

You don't need red meat to make a hearty stew. You just need a few beans, some flavorful vegetables, and of course, lots of wine! While the stew simmers, revel in the sweet bouquet of flavors that escape all around you. **Serves 6**

I N G R E D I E N T S

1 ½ tablespoons extra-virgin olive oil

1 large onion, chopped

3 cloves garlic, sliced

1 (29-ounce) can tomato puree

1 large russet potato, diced

2 carrots, chopped

2 cups dry red wine

1 ½ cups cooked dark red kidney beans, drained, or 1 (15-ounce) can dark red kidney beans, drained and rinsed

1 ½ cups cooked large butter beans, drained, or 1 (15-ounce) can large butter beans, drained and rinsed

1 (6-ounce) can whole black olives, drained

1 (16-ounce) can whole pearl onions, drained

M E T H O D

In a large pot, heat olive oil over medium heat. Add onion and garlic and sauté until onion is translucent.

Add tomato puree, potato, carrots, wine, beans, olives, and pearl onions and bring to a boil.

Reduce heat to medium-low and simmer about 30 minutes, or until carrots and potatoes are tender.

Serve hot, with sourdough French bread.

BlackBean
CubanBake

You don't have to sail to Havana to enjoy Cuban cuisine. Just take that short trip to your kitchen and whip up my Black Bean Cuban Bake. It's both spicy and sweet, with seasoned bread crumbs supplying a wonderful mealy texture.

Serves 4

I N G R E D I E N T S

3 cups cooked black beans, drained, or 2 (15-ounce) cans black beans, drained and rinsed

1 medium onion, chopped

1/2 cup chopped bell pepper

1 (8¾-ounce) can whole-kernel corn, drained

1/4 cup seasoned bread crumbs

2 tablespoons catsup

1 tablespoon prepared mustard

2 tablespoons brown sugar

1/2 teaspoon ground cumin

M E T H O D

Preheat oven to 350°F.

In a 2-quart casserole, combine all ingredients and mix well.

Cover and bake 1 hour, stirring once after 40 minutes.

Serve immediately.

Kidney Bean Turkey Loaf

If baseball is America's favorite pastime, then eating my Kidney Bean Turkey Loaf should be number 2. I've taken a pound of ground turkey and stretched it to twice its volume just by adding a few dark red kidney beans and some chopped onion! It's great with a bottle of red wine.

Serves 4 to 6

INGREDIENTS

1 cup cooked dark red kidney beans, drained and chopped, or 1 cup canned dark red kidney beans, drained, rinsed, and chopped

1 pound ground turkey breast

1 small onion, chopped

½ cup pasta sauce (any kind)

1 teaspoon black pepper

1 teaspoon Dijon mustard

Preheat oven to 350°F.

In a 9 × 5 × 3-inch nonstick loaf pan, combine all ingredients and mix well.

Bake 45 minutes, or until done.

Enjoy with lots of catsup!

PastaBean Supreme

Every Wednesday night is pasta night at my place. Friends drive from all over to taste my Pasta Bean Supreme, an enticing entree of penne pasta basking in my exquisite butter bean sauce enhanced with sautéd garlic and red onion slices. **Serves 2**

I N G R E D I E N T S

2 cups penne pasta

1 tablespoon extra-virgin olive oil

3 cloves garlic, sliced

1 small red onion, sliced into thin rings

¾ cup pasta sauce (any kind)

1½ cups cooked large butter beans, drained, or 1 (15-ounce) can large butter beans, drained and rinsed

2 small Roma (plum) tomatoes, chopped

M E T H O D

In a large pot of boiling salted water, cook pasta al dente.

Meanwhile, in a large skillet, heat olive oil over medium heat. Add garlic and onion rings and sauté until onion becomes limp.

Add pasta sauce, beans, and tomatoes to skillet and cook, stirring occasionally, until heated through.

Transfer cooked, drained pasta to skillet and toss.

Serve immediately with red wine and candlelight.

Fava Balls

Fava Balls are so flavorful, you'll never serve a meatball again! There are many good things packed into them: red bell pepper, parsley, Parmesan cheese, green onions, and garlic. Come to think of it, everything that's growing in my backyard is in these balls. Enjoy! **Makes 15 balls**

I N G R E D I E N T S

2 cups cooked fava beans, drained, or 1 (19-ounce) can fava beans, drained and rinsed

1 tablespoon extra-virgin olive oil

1 cup finely chopped red bell pepper

2 green onions, finely chopped

1 clove garlic, minced

1 tablespoon finely chopped fresh parsley

½ cup freshly shredded Parmesan cheese

½ cup plain bread crumbs

M E T H O D

In a large bowl, mash fava beans.

In a large nonstick skillet, heat olive oil over medium heat. Add bell pepper, green onions, garlic, and parsley and sauté until bell pepper is tender and limp.

Transfer bell pepper mixture to bowl of beans. Add cheese and bread crumbs and mix well. Form into medium-size balls.

Return skillet to stove and place balls in skillet. Heat over medium-low heat for about 7 minutes, or until balls are warmed through. If you prefer, heat them on the barbecue instead!

Serve immediately with barbecue sauce or catsup and a favorite vegetable.

Barbecued Pinquitos

Flavorful pinquitos taste even better prepared with a little onion and some barbecue sauce. Simply spoon over rice and you've got a delicious protein-filled dinner. You can use pink beans if you prefer. **Serves 4**

I N G R E D I E N T S

1 tablespoon extra-virgin olive oil

1 small onion, chopped

1 cup barbecue sauce

1 ½ cups cooked pinquito beans or pink beans, drained, or 1 (15-ounce) can pinquito beans, drained and rinsed

¼ teaspoon garlic powder

3 cups cooked brown rice

M E T H O D

In a medium saucepan, heat olive oil over medium heat. Add onion and sauté until translucent.

Add barbecue sauce, beans, and garlic powder and cook, stirring occasionally, until heated through.

Spoon mixture over rice and serve immediately.

CHAPTER FOUR

"Second Beananas" Sidekick Dishes

Behind every successful main dish is a tempting side dish. And if you don't believe me, just take a whiff of the likes of Gorgeous Black-eyes, Pintos in Cheddar, Beans Teriyaki, and Amazing Limas and Chorizo.

Enjoy a sizzling steak accompanied by my Incredible Edible Mashed Bean Potatoes. The potatoes are blended with hearty mashed garbanzo beans, Cheddar cheese, olives, and chives and seasoned with garlic powder, paprika, and white pepper. They're irresistible.

Or how about my Pesto Cannellini? Its sweet basil flavor goes great with all of your favorite pasta recipes.

Having grilled chicken for dinner? Try my easy-to-make Pintos in Cheddar with a glass of wine. Or if you're going south of the border, serve up my spicy Fat-Free Refried Beans to go along with your scrumptious burrito.

For picnics and holidays I recommend my cold Potato Bean Salad and my Black Bean Pasta Salad. Either tastes great with my classic Pinto Patties.

If you're in the market for an alternative to your high-fat Thanksgiving stuffing, my Bean Stuffing fits the bill perfectly. Gone is the yucky saturated fat of sausage!

Now, if you're a fish lover you'll fall for my Spaghetti Squash and Kidney Beans accented with pasta sauce, fresh cilantro, garlic powder, and Parmesan cheese—it's great with any kind of seafood.

Whatever you're having as your main course, you'll find that one of my yummy and attractive side dishes is a perfect match.

RanchHandBeans

I call these Ranch Hand Beans because they're perfect for the ranch hands in your family who need lots of energy and protein! Steak sauce enhances the flavors of the pinto beans, ground beef, and Roma tomatoes, making this a sensational sweet-and-sour side dish.   **Serves 8**

I N G R E D I E N T S

1 pound ground beef

1 small onion, finely chopped

4 Roma (plum) tomatoes, chopped

½ cup steak sauce

1 ½ cups cooked pinto beans, drained, or 1 (15-ounce)
can pinto beans, drained and rinsed

M E T H O D

In a large skillet, brown ground beef along with onion and tomatoes over medium heat just until tender. Drain off excess liquid.

Add steak sauce and beans and cook for about 10 minutes, until beans are heated through.

Serve immediately.

P̱estoC̱annellini

If you have the choice between making Pesto Cannellini and
making love, you'll choose Pesto Cannellini any day! There's
nothing like the aroma of sweet basil in homemade pesto.
After you try this recipe, I guarantee you'll want to smoke a
cigarette.   **Serves 4**

I   N   G   R   E   D   I   E   N   T   S

3 cups cooked cannellini beans, drained, or 2 (15-ounce)
cans cannellini beans, drained and rinsed

2 cups lightly packed fresh basil

½ cup extra-virgin olive oil

4 large cloves garlic, peeled

½ cup freshly shredded Parmesan cheese

3 tablespoons freshly shredded Romano cheese

M E T H O D

Place beans in a large bowl.

In a blender or food processor, combine remaining ingredients and puree until smooth. Pour pureed mixture into bowl of beans and fold in.

Transfer mixture to a nonstick skillet and heat over medium heat, turning once.

Serve immediately, and try to control yourself!

IncredibleEdible MashedBean Potatoes

I can't stand wasting food, so the potato pulp that I scooped out of the baked potatoes I used to make my Baked Bean Potato Skins was turned into a scrumptious recipe all by itself. **Serves 6 to 8**

I N G R E D I E N T S

3 cups baked potato pulp

1½ cups cooked garbanzo beans, drained and mashed, or 1 (15-ounce) can garbanzo beans, drained, rinsed, and mashed

1 cup shredded Cheddar cheese

1 (2¼-ounce) can sliced black olives, drained

2 tablespoons chopped chives

¼ teaspoon garlic powder

¼ teaspoon paprika

¼ teaspoon white pepper

M E T H O D

Preheat oven to 400°F.

In a medium casserole, combine all ingredients and mix thoroughly. Cover and bake approximately 20 minutes.

Serve immediately.

Fat-Free
RefriedBeans

We all love refried beans, but unfortunately many of the canned brands we buy contain lard. So I've come up with a recipe that is virtually fat-free and cholesterol-free. Enjoy its lively flavor of fresh cilantro and fresh lime juice.

Serves 2

I N G R E D I E N T S

2 tablespoons seasoned rice vinegar

⅓ cup finely chopped onion

½ teaspoon ground cumin

1 teaspoon minced garlic

½ teaspoon finely chopped fresh cilantro

Pinch cayenne pepper

1½ cups cooked pinto beans, drained, or 1 (15-ounce) can pinto beans, drained and rinsed

½ cup warm water

2 teaspoons freshly squeezed lime juice

M E T H O D

In a medium saucepan, heat rice vinegar over medium heat. Add onion and sauté until soft.

Stir in cumin, garlic, cilantro, and cayenne pepper and cook for about 30 seconds.

Add beans and stir in water. Cook until water is absorbed.

Remove from heat and stir in lime juice.

Serve immediately.

BeanStuffing

Get rid of all that fattening sausage in your turkey stuffing! Use beans instead! I like butter beans, black beans, and garbanzo beans, but feel free to experiment with your own favorite beans.

Makes enough to stuff the biggest bird, and then some

I N G R E D I E N T S

½ cup butter

1 large onion, chopped

2 cloves garlic, minced

2 stalks celery, chopped

2 cups mixed cooked large butter beans, black beans, and garbanzo beans, drained, or 2 cups mixed canned large butter beans, black beans, and garbanzo beans, drained and rinsed

3 cups seasoned bread cubes

⅓ cup chicken broth

1 teaspoon dried oregano

¼ teaspoon black pepper

M E T H O D

In a large skillet, melt butter over medium-low heat. Add onion, garlic, and celery and sauté until onion is tender.

Add beans and bread cubes and stir in chicken broth. (If you prefer a moister stuffing, add additional chicken broth.) Sprinkle in oregano and pepper and stir to blend.

Allow mixture to cool, then stuff your bird!

 Black Bean
Stir-fry

Stir-frying isn't just for vegetables . . . it's for beans too! The sesame oil provides the Asian flavor of the dish and enriches the taste of all the appetizing ingredients.   **Serves 6**

I N G R E D I E N T S

¼ cup seasoned rice vinegar

2 tablespoons soy sauce

1 tablespoon dry sherry

1 tablespoon sesame oil

1 cup grated carrot

1 cup grated onion

1 clove garlic, minced

3 cups cooked black beans, drained, or 2 (15-ounce) cans black beans, drained and rinsed

½ teaspoon chili powder

¼ teaspoon ground cumin

M E T H O D

In a small bowl, combine rice vinegar, soy sauce, and sherry.

In a large nonstick skillet, heat sesame oil over high heat. Add carrot, onion, and garlic and stir-fry for about 1 minute.

Add beans, vinegar mixture, chili powder, and cumin. Continue to stir-fry about 3 minutes until mixture reduces and beans are heated through.

Serve as a side dish or as a main course over rice.

Gorgeous
Black-eyes

When I was first developing this recipe, I looked in the skillet and thought, "Wow! These black-eyes are gorgeous!" Prepared in a base of barbecue sauce with corn, chopped tomatoes, and peppers, it's one side dish that will leave your guests wanting more. **Serves 6 to 8**

I N G R E D I E N T S

½ cup barbecue sauce

3 cups cooked black-eyed peas, drained, or 2 (15-ounce) cans black-eyed peas, drained and rinsed

1 cup chopped Roma (plum) tomatoes

1 (8¾-ounce) can whole-kernel corn, drained

⅓ cup chopped green bell pepper

½ teaspoon garlic powder

½ cup shredded mozzarella cheese

M E T H O D

In a large skillet, combine all ingredients except mozzarella cheese over medium heat and cook, stirring occasionally, for about 10 minutes.

Turn off heat. Sprinkle cheese over top of mixture.

When cheese melts, serve immediately.

Potato Bean Salad

I've taken an American favorite and made it my own! I've added dark red kidney beans, and I've gotten rid of the fatty mayonnaise by substituting nonfat yogurt. Come on, what are you waiting for? Give it a try! **Serves 8**

INGREDIENTS

3½ cups boiled and diced red potatoes, unpeeled (about 7 small potatoes)

1½ cups cooked dark red kidney beans, drained, or 1 (15-ounce) can dark red kidney beans, drained and rinsed

¾ cup plain nonfat yogurt

½ cup finely chopped red onion

1 (2¼-ounce) can sliced black olives, drained

2 tablespoons finely chopped fresh parsley

½ teaspoon chopped fresh dill

¼ teaspoon garlic powder

¼ teaspoon salt

METHOD

In a large bowl, combine all ingredients and toss gently.

Refrigerate for a couple of hours and serve chilled.

Spaghetti Squash and Kidney Beans

Spaghetti squash is a lot of fun to prepare. Once it is cooked, I love to take a fork and flake off the strands of "spaghetti." This squash usually has a bland taste, but when combined with red kidney beans, pasta sauce, garlic powder, cilantro, and Parmesan cheese, it takes on a delicious new identity!

Serves 6 to 8

I N G R E D I E N T S

4 cups cooked spaghetti squash

1 ½ cups cooked dark red kidney beans, drained, or 1 (15-ounce) can dark red kidney beans, drained and rinsed

1 cup pasta sauce (any kind)

1 teaspoon chopped fresh cilantro

½ teaspoon garlic powder

½ cup freshly shredded Parmesan cheese

M E T H O D

In a 3-quart saucepan, combine all ingredients except cheese over medium heat. Cook, stirring occasionally, until heated through.

Remove from heat, stir in cheese, and serve immediately.

Amazing Limas and Chorizo

Spicy side dishes are always a favorite of mine. Chorizo sausage, although full of fat, adds a special zip to the combination of baby lima beans, onions, and corn. The flavor is heightened with a touch of mellow seasoned rice vinegar. Wonderful with chicken fajitas! **Serves 6 to 8**

I N G R E D I E N T S

1 pound beef chorizo

½ cup seasoned rice vinegar

1 cup chopped onion

1 (8¾-ounce) can whole-kernel corn, drained

2 cups cooked baby lima beans, drained, or 1 (10-ounce) package frozen baby lima beans, thawed

M E T H O D

In a large skillet, brown chorizo over medium heat. Drain off excess grease.

Return skillet to stove and add rice vinegar, onion, corn, and beans. Cook for about 10 minutes.

Serve immediately.

Pintos in Cheddar

This is a mouthwatering cheesy side dish that will complement that pork chop or hot, sizzling steak you've got cooking on the grill! **Serves 4**

INGREDIENTS

1 tablespoon extra-virgin olive oil

1 small onion, chopped

1 cup tomato and basil pasta sauce

1 1/2 cups cooked pinto beans, drained, or 1 (15-ounce) can pinto beans, drained and rinsed

1/2 cup shredded Cheddar cheese

METHOD

In a 3-quart saucepan, heat olive oil over medium heat. Add onion and sauté until tender.

Stir in pasta sauce and beans and cook, stirring occasionally, until heated through.

Add cheese and stir until melted.

Serve immediately.

Black Bean Pasta Salad

Black Bean Pasta Salad is a simple cold salad you can take along on a picnic or to the beach. The attractive rainbow rotini pasta makes it very colorful, and the creamy ranch dressing provides a wonderful flavor. Perfect for Labor Day or the 4th of July!

Serves 8

INGREDIENTS

2 cups rainbow rotini pasta

1 (8¾-ounce) can whole-kernel corn, drained

1 carrot, grated

⅔ cup grated onion

1 teaspoon chopped fresh dill

1 cup fat-free ranch dressing

1½ cups cooked black beans, drained, or 1 (15-ounce) can black beans, drained and rinsed

METHOD

Cook pasta al dente, according to package directions.

Transfer pasta to a large glass bowl. Add remaining ingredients and mix well.

Refrigerate for a couple of hours and serve chilled.

BeansTeriyaki

Great Northerns are fabulous in a glaze of teriyaki sauce along with sautéd onion and a hint of cilantro. I enjoy Beans Teriyaki with all of my chicken dishes.   **Serves 4**

I N G R E D I E N T S

1 teaspoon extra-virgin olive oil

½ cup chopped red onion

3 cups cooked Great Northern beans, drained, or 2 (15-ounce) cans Great Northern beans, drained and rinsed

⅓ cup teriyaki sauce

1 teaspoon chopped fresh cilantro

M E T H O D

In a large skillet, heat olive oil over medium heat.

Add onion and sauté until tender.

Add beans and stir in teriyaki sauce. Add cilantro and cook until beans are heated through.

Serve immediately.

CHAPTER FIVE

"Temptation Sensations" Dazzling Desserts

In the beginning, Adam and Eve were tempted by the apple. Nowadays, we're all tempted by delicious desserts. We love them, but we feel guilty about eating them because they're full of nasty fat and calories.

Well, I, for one, don't feel guilty at all because by adding beans to my favorite desserts, I'm adding healthy fiber, protein, and vitamins.

My Flaming Black Bean Jubilee will surprise and astound your guests. This sweet combination of black beans, raisins, and flaming brandy is delicious over vanilla ice cream. It's a wonderful treat!

Want a quick recipe for cheesecake? No problem. My Kidney Bean Cheesecake is so elegant that your guests will think you're a gourmet chef.

For the holidays, try my Minty Bean Chocolate Squares. I use mashed garbanzo beans instead of nuts and a little mint extract for a unique flavor.

Don't forget my Jelly Bean Love Drops. Make these colorful drop cookies with cherry-flavored jelly beans for Valentine's Day or for your kids and grandkids. They'll love 'em!

Oh, if only Adam and Eve had a second chance, they could be enjoying Pumpkin Bean Pie, Chocolate Mousse with Beans, Carrot Bean Cupcakes, and of course, my Chocolate-Covered Garbanzo Balls!

Chocolate-Covered GarbanzoBalls

It doesn't get any simpler than this. Chocolate-Covered Garbanzo Balls! Just mash a can of garbanzo beans, then use your hands to form the mashed beans into little balls and dip into chocolate! A wonderful, quick, nutty dessert.

Makes 18 balls

I N G R E D I E N T S

1½ cups cooked garbanzo beans, drained, or 1 (15-ounce) can garbanzo beans, drained and rinsed

8 ounces semisweet or sweet baking chocolate

M E T H O D

In a blender or food processor, puree beans. With your clean hands, roll bean puree into 18 small balls.

In a saucepan, melt chocolate over low heat.

Place 1 ball on top of a salad fork. Gently lower into chocolate so that ball is completely submerged and bathe until thoroughly coated. Slide fork underneath ball and carefully remove and place on a nonstick baking sheet. Repeat this step until all balls are coated in chocolate.

Refrigerate balls for about 2 hours and serve chilled.

Flaming Black Bean Jubilee

The perfect dessert to end all meals, this will amaze your dinner guests. Sweet candied black beans and raisins dance under flaming brandy—magnificent! **Serves 6**

I N G R E D I E N T S

1 ½ cups cooked black beans, drained, or 1 (15-ounce) can black beans, drained and rinsed

1 cup sugar

¼ cup raisins

¼ teaspoon ground allspice

¼ cup water

Vanilla ice cream

½ cup brandy

M E T H O D

In a 2-quart saucepan, combine all ingredients except ice cream and brandy. Mix and bring to a rapid boil. Stir continuously until mixture becomes moderately thick, about 10 minutes. Remove from heat.

Scoop ice cream into desert bowls. Fill a ladle with brandy and hold over a burner until brandy becomes warm. Ignite brandy and pour into bean mixture. Stir until flame is extinguished.

Ladle mixture over the ice cream and serve immediately.

Kidney Bean Cheesecake

This cheesecake is like no other cheesecake in the world. The cheese mixture develops a red tint and unique texture as the cream cheese blends with the mashed dark red kidney beans. The flavor is out of this world. Kidney Bean Cheesecake is not as fattening as other cheesecakes because it's made with reduced-fat cream cheese. **Serves 8**

I N G R E D I E N T S

1½ cups cooked dark red kidney beans, drained, or 1 (15-ounce) can dark red kidney beans, drained and rinsed

2 (8-ounce) packages reduced-fat cream cheese

½ cup sugar

½ teaspoon vanilla extract

¼ teaspoon ground cinnamon

1 large egg white

1 (9-inch) ready-to-use graham cracker crumb pie shell

M E T H O D

Preheat oven to 350°F.

In a large bowl, mash beans with a spoon or with your clean hands.

Add remaining ingredients except pie shell and mix with an electric mixer on medium speed.

Pour mixture into pie shell. Bake 40 minutes, or until center is just about set.

Remove from oven and let cool on a wire rack, then refrigerate for 4 hours.

Serve chilled.

Chocolate Mousse with Beans

Once, when I was to cook on a television show, I was told that Julia Child would be on too. So I took a look at Julia's cookbook *The Way to Cook* and found a delicious recipe for chocolate mousse. There was only one thing wrong with it—it didn't have beans! So I fixed it and gave it some fiber. Julia loved it! **Serves 6**

I N G R E D I E N T S

8 ounces semisweet baking chocolate

6 tablespoons butter, softened

3 large egg yolks

¼ cup strong brewed coffee

⅓ cup cooked Great Northern beans, drained and mashed, or ⅓ cup canned Great Northern beans, drained, rinsed, and mashed

3 large egg whites

¼ cup finely ground sugar

1 cup heavy cream, whipped

1 can "real" whipped cream

M E T H O D

In a large saucepan, melt chocolate over low heat.

Remove from heat and beat in butter, egg yolks, coffee, and beans.

In a large bowl, beat egg whites into soft peaks, then spoon sugar into bowl as you beat into stiff peaks.

Pour chocolate mixture down side of bowl and fold in to egg whites. Fold in whipped cream.

Pour mixture into wineglasses. Cover and refrigerate for about 2 hours, or until firm.

Remove from refrigerator and top with canned whipped cream. Instead of a cherry, top each serving with a bean!

CarrotBean Cupcakes

Having trouble getting the little ones to eat their beans? Well, these terrific Carrot Bean Cupcakes made with jarred baby food carrots and pureed pinto beans are the answer to your prayers. They taste great, and your kids won't even know they're grazing on beans! See, you *can* have your cake and eat it too! **Makes 24 cupcakes**

INGREDIENTS

2 cups all-purpose flour

2 cups granulated sugar

1 teaspoon baking powder

1 teaspoon baking soda

1 teaspoon salt

1 teaspoon ground cinnamon

½ cup butter, softened

3 (4-ounce) jars baby food pureed carrots

1½ cups cooked pinto beans, drained and pureed, or 1 (15-ounce) can pinto beans drained, rinsed, and pureed

3 large egg whites

1 cup raisins

M   E   T   H   O   D

Preheat oven to 325°F. Place cupcake liners in two 12-cup muffin pans.

In a large bowl, combine flour, sugar, baking powder, baking soda, salt, and cinnamon.

Add butter, carrots, beans, and egg whites. Beat with an electric mixer until smooth. Fold in raisins.

Spoon mixture almost to the top of each cupcake liner and bake for about 30 minutes, or until cupcakes are lightly browned and have begun to pull away from sides of pan.

Let cool on a wire rack, then frost with Pinto Bean Frosting (recipe follows).

Pinto Bean Frosting

This is the perfect "3-ingredient" frosting to top all of your cakes and cupcakes. Who would have thought you could have fiber in frosting?!

Makes enough to cover 2 (9-inch) cakes

INGREDIENTS

1 (3-ounce) package reduced-fat cream cheese

1 cup cooked pinto beans, drained and pureed, or 1 cup canned pinto beans, drained, rinsed, and pureed

3 cups confectioners' sugar

METHOD

In a large bowl, combine all ingredients and beat together with an electric mixer.

Spread over cooled cakes or cupcakes.

Minty Bean Chocolate Squares

Way back when, in the Mediterranean countries, garbanzo beans were used as an aphrodisiac. In this country, chocolate is said to make the heart grow fonder too. I use both ingredients in my Garbanzo Bean Chocolate Squares, but the only thing I guarantee is that you'll fall in love with this recipe. **Makes about 2½ pounds of squares**

I N G R E D I E N T S

4 ounces unsweetened baking chocolate

1 cup butter

1½ cups cooked garbanzo beans, drained and mashed, or 1 (15-ounce) can garbanzo beans, drained, rinsed, and mashed

2½ tablespoons mint extract

2 pounds confectioners' sugar

continued

Butter a 13 × 9 × 2-inch baking pan.

In a large saucepan, melt chocolate and butter over low heat.

Remove from heat and mix in garbanzos, mint extract, and confectioners' sugar.

Pour mixture into buttered baking pan and refrigerate until hard.

Remove from refrigerator and cut into squares.

Pop squares in your mouth!

Kidney Bean Cream Cheese Holiday Cookies

The holidays are a time for joy and a time for beans. There's nothing like sitting in front of the fire with a glass of milk and my Kidney Bean Cream Cheese Holiday Cookies. The flecks of the mashed dark red kidney bean skins add terrific holiday color and texture.

Makes about 4 dozen cookies

1 (8-ounce) package cream cheese, softened

½ cup butter, softened

1 cup granulated sugar

1 ½ cups all-purpose flour

1 cup cooked dark red kidney beans, drained and mashed, or 1 cup canned dark red kidney beans, drained, rinsed, and mashed

Colored sprinkles

M E T H O D

In a large bowl, blend all ingredients except colored sprinkles.

Divide mixture in fourths and roll into balls. Cover each ball with plastic wrap and refrigerate overnight.

Preheat oven to 350°F.

Roll out dough on a floured pastry cloth or other floured surface to ⅛-inch thickness. Using cookie cutters, cut dough into shapes such as trees, reindeer, stars, and bells.

Place cookies on ungreased cookie sheets 1 inch apart. Decorate with sprinkles.

Bake for 6 to 8 minutes. Let cool on wire racks. Serve with a tall, frosty glass of milk.

Pumpkin Bean Pie

You won't want to wait until Thanksgiving to make this pie.
My Pumpkin Bean Pie packs a double wallop of fiber . . .
fiber from the pumpkin and fiber from the beans. Now that's
something to be thankful for!   **Serves 8**

I N G R E D I E N T S

1 (16-ounce) can pumpkin

1½ cups cooked Great Northern beans, drained and
pureed, or 1 (15-ounce) can Great Northern beans,
drained, rinsed, and pureed

2 large egg whites

¾ cup granulated sugar

2 teaspoons ground cinnamon

1 teaspoon ground ginger

1 teaspoon ground cloves

¼ teaspoon ground nutmeg

¼ teaspoon ground allspice

1 (9-inch) ready-to-use pie crust

M E T H O D

Preheat oven to 425° F.

In a large bowl, combine all ingredients except pie crust, and mix thoroughly with an electric mixer.

Pour mixture into pie crust and smooth filling with a knife or spatula.

Bake at 425° F for 15 minutes. Reduce heat to 325° F and bake an additional 50 minutes to 1 hour, or until a knife inserted in the center comes out clean.

Serve warm or at room temperature.

Jelly Bean Love Drops

How could I write a cookbook and not include everybody's favorite bean, the jelly bean! A batch of my Jelly Bean Love Drops makes a delectable delight and the perfect gift for your lover on Valentine's Day. **Makes 36 love drops**

INGREDIENTS

1 ¼ cups all-purpose flour

½ teaspoon baking soda

½ teaspoon salt

¼ cup butter, softened

½ cup granulated sugar

¼ cup dark brown sugar

2 large egg whites

1 teaspoon vanilla extract

½ cup cherry-flavored mini jelly beans

M E T H O D

Preheat oven to 375°F.

In a large bowl, combine flour, baking soda, and salt.

Add butter, sugars, egg whites, and vanilla and beat well. Fold in jelly beans.

On a nonstick or greased cookie sheet, drop rounded tea-spoons of mixture 2 inches apart.

Bake 8 to 10 minutes.

Let cool on wire racks.

Bean Gelatin Royale

Whenever I was sick and didn't go to school, my mom, Dolores, would make a gelatin dessert for me. It was so boring, and when she'd set it down in front of me, it wiggled and made me feel sicker. Well, I couldn't take it anymore, so I invented a gelatin recipe that makes me happy and well. I spiked lemon gelatin with crème de menthe. Now when it wiggles, I'm entertained by the dancing kidney beans inside.

Serves 8

INGREDIENTS

1 (6-ounce) box lemon gelatin

3 tablespoons crème de menthe

½ cup cooked dark red kidney beans, drained, or
½ cup canned dark red kidney beans, drained and rinsed

METHOD

Prepare gelatin according to package directions.

Stir in crème de menthe and refrigerate.

When gelatin starts to thicken, stir in beans.

Return to refrigerator until firm; serve chilled.

The Bean Clubhouse Glossary

Black Beans: Black beans are also known as turtle beans, *frijoles negros,* and Spanish black beans. Like their relative the pinto bean, black beans are from South America. Some feel black beans have a slight mushroom taste, but I would have to disagree because I hate mushrooms but love black beans.

Black-eyed Peas: These peas are really beans! They're cream-colored, with black keels, and they have a wonderful savory flavor.

Cannellini Beans: These beans are also known as white kidney beans. Their texture is smooth and they have a nutty flavor. Originally grown in Argentina, they're very popular in Italian dishes.

Fava Beans: Favas, also known as broad beans, are large beans with a bitter taste. They are the only bean indigenous to Europe.

Garbanzo Beans: The garbanzo bean looks like a ram's head. Garbanzos have a nutty flavor and are also known as chick-peas and ceci beans.

Great Northern Beans: Great Northerns weren't named for the North Pole (at least, I think they weren't), but they look almost snow white. They are actually the mature seeds of green beans. They have a very mild flavor.

Green Beans: Green beans are harvested and consumed, pod and all, when they are immature and tender. Varieties include string beans, snap beans, and snow peas.

Kidney Beans: Kidney beans are available dark red, light red, and white (cannellini). As their name implies, they're shaped like a kidney. They have a terrific rich flavor and look good in every recipe. These beans are very photogenic.

Lentils: The lentil is probably the oldest legume on the face of the earth, dating from 7000 B.C. It's also one of the smallest, about ¼ inch round. The Egyptians, Greeks, and Romans ate them, so they're good enough for me!

Lima Beans: These creamy white to pale green beans are also known as butter beans. There are two main species of this flattish bean—the large lima and the baby lima. The large lima was born in Central America and later traveled to Peru and is named for its capital. The baby lima was raised in Mexico. I can't begin to describe the taste . . . only that I love 'em.

Navy Beans: Navy beans are small, white, and oval. They are named after the U.S. Navy because they've long been a part of the Navy diet. They're most often used in canned versions of baked beans, pork and beans, and vegetarian beans.

Pink Beans: The pink version of the red bean is used in South American dishes. I sometimes like to use them in place of pinquito beans. Some cooks like to interchange them with pinto beans.

Pinquito Beans: Harvested in California, pinquitos are small, with a pinkish brown tint. They have great flavor and are a favorite at barbecues.

Pinto Beans: The pinto bean hails from South America. Its skin, tan in color, is streaked with pink and brown markings. That's why it's named for the Spanish word for "spotted." It is very flavorful and is used in many South American and Mexican dishes.

Red Beans: Reds are medium-sized oval beans. They are maroon in color. If you live in or visit the South, you know them well, as they're used traditionally in Creole dishes such as red beans and rice. They're also interchangeable with red kidney beans.

Small White Beans: These beans resemble the navy bean but are a little smaller and firmer. Small white beans, navy beans, and Great Northern beans can all be used interchangeably.

Index